C0-EDZ-429

600565
21.50

SNAKES

SNAKES

600565

PETER MURRAY

THE CHILD'S WORLD

7484

PHOTO RESEARCH
Charles Rotter/Gary Lopez Productions

PHOTO CREDITS
Joe McDonald: front cover,
back cover, 2, 6-7, 13, 15, 19, 25
Comstock/Russ Kinne: 9, 27, 29, 31
Comstock/Comstock: 11
Comstock/George Lepp: 17
Comstock/Gwen Fidler: 21
Robert and Linda Mitchell: 23

Text Copyright © 1992 by The Child's World, Inc.
All rights reserved. No part of this book may be
reproduced or utilized in any form or by any means
without written permission from the Publisher.
Printed in the United States of America.

Distributed to schools and libraries in the United States by
ENCYCLOPAEDIA BRITANNICA EDUCATIONAL CORP.
310 South Michigan Avenue
Chicago, Illinois 60604

Library of Congress Cataloging-in-Publication Data
Murray, Peter, 1952 Sept. 29-
Snakes / by Peter Murray.
p. cm.
Summary: Introduces the physical and behavioral
characteristics of a variety of snakes.
ISBN 0-89565-849-6

1. Snakes--Juvenile literature. [1. Snakes.]	I. Title.
QL666.06M85 1992	91-39710
597.96--dc20	CIP
	AC

CONTENTS

Introduction 6

Boa Constrictors 8

Pythons 10

Anacondas 12

Garter Snakes 14

Vine Snakes 16

Copperheads 18

Cottonmouths 20

Rattlesnakes 22

Puff Adders 24

Cobras 26

Mambas 28

Coral Snakes 30

Snakes live in almost every country in the world. There are about 3,000 different kinds of snakes. The anaconda is so big it can swallow a pig. Thread snakes are only a few inches long. Some snakes are brightly colored. Others are so well camouflaged they are hard to see.

Like crocodiles, lizards, and turtles, snakes are reptiles. All reptiles are cold-blooded. Their body temperature rises and falls depending on the temperature of their surroundings. Reptiles are active in warm weather, but they hibernate when the temperature drops.

Snakes have dry, scaly skin. Many have beautiful colors and patterns, like the one in this photograph. Snakes do not have legs, so they use the scales on their bellies to pull themselves along. All snakes have forked tongues that they use to feel and to pick up odors. Some snakes produce a poison called *venom*. When poisonous snakes bite their prey, they inject it with venom, killing it quickly.

Many people are afraid of snakes. Some snakes are dangerous, but most are harmless to people. They are an important part of nature and help us by eating rats, mice, and other pests.

BOA CONSTRICTORS

Boa constrictors are large, strong snakes that are found all over South America, Africa, and Asia. Boa constrictors move slowly through the trees or in the water. When a boa sees a small animal, it grabs it with its sharp teeth. The snake then wraps its long, strong body around its victim and squeezes until the animal is dead. This is why they are called constrictors. The boa swallows its meal whole. An adult boa can swallow animals that are twice as big around as its own body! Boa constrictors are not poisonous, and sometimes they are kept as pets.

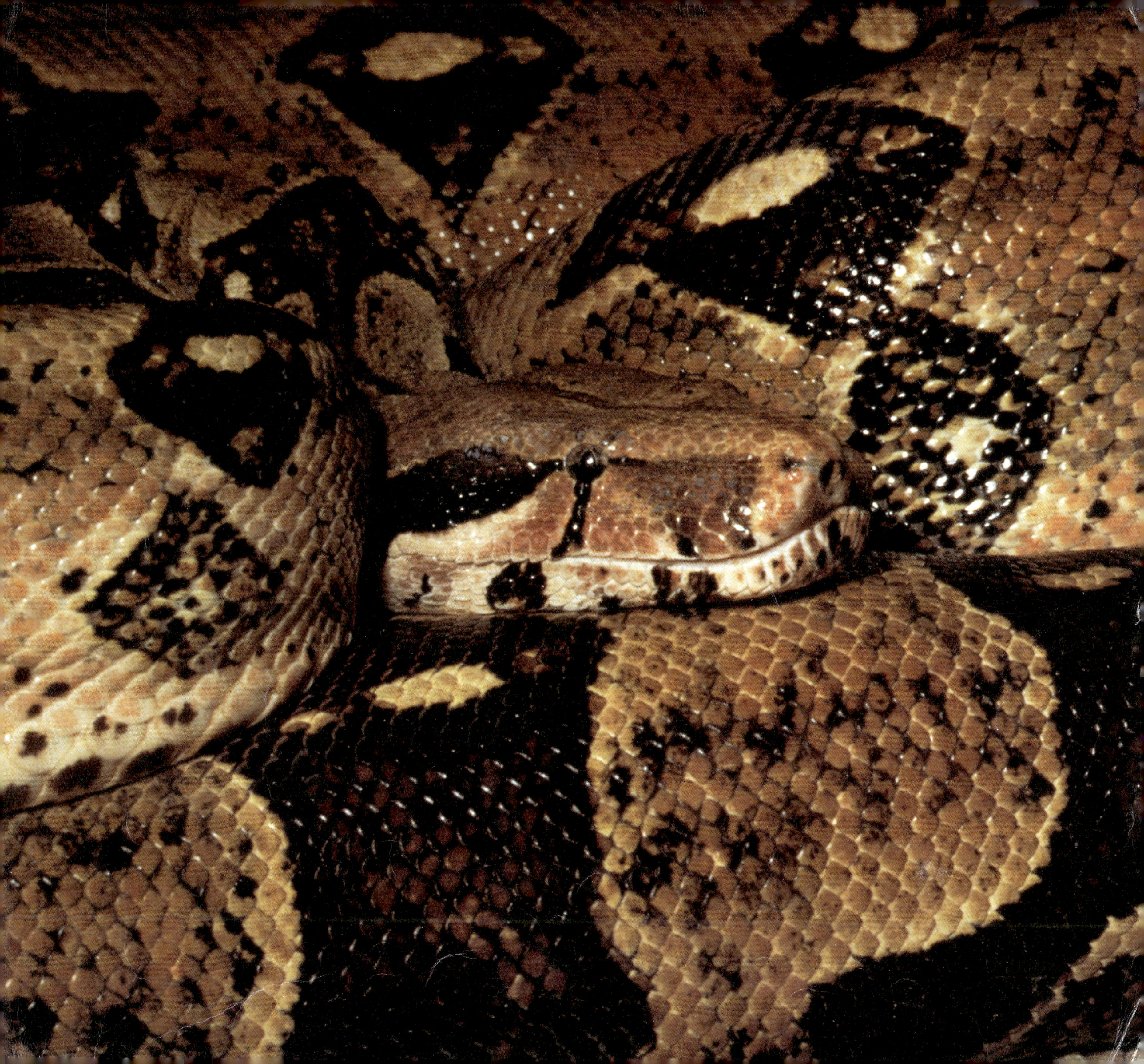

PYTHONS

Pythons are close relatives of boa constrictors. They usually live in trees or near water. A python kills its prey by wrapping its body around the animal and squeezing. Both pythons and boa constrictors have heat-sensing pits under their eyes. The snakes sense the body heat of their prey, so they can hunt even in complete darkness. There are many different kinds of pythons. The biggest of all is the *reticulated python*. The longest snake ever measured was a 33-foot reticulated python that was found in the Philippines. It was nearly as long as a school bus!

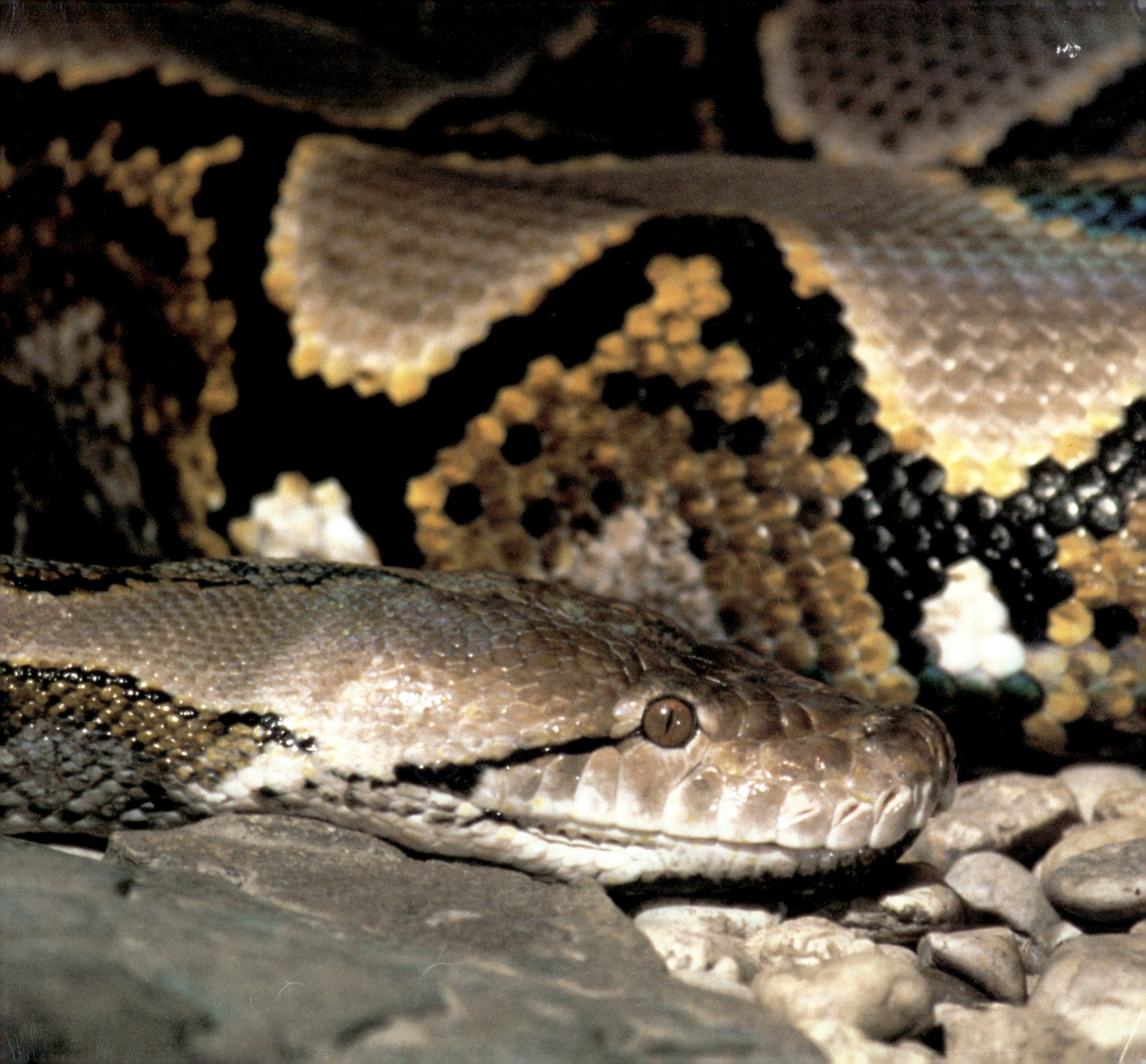

ANACONDAS

The South American anaconda is the biggest snake in the world. Its body is much thicker and heavier than that of the tree-dwelling reticulated python. The biggest anaconda ever measured was over 28 feet long. The anaconda is a member of the boa constrictor family. The anaconda likes to stay in the water. It feeds on animals that it finds near the banks of rivers. Anacondas have been known to swallow large mammals such as pigs. They will even capture and eat the alligator-like caimans that live in South American rivers.

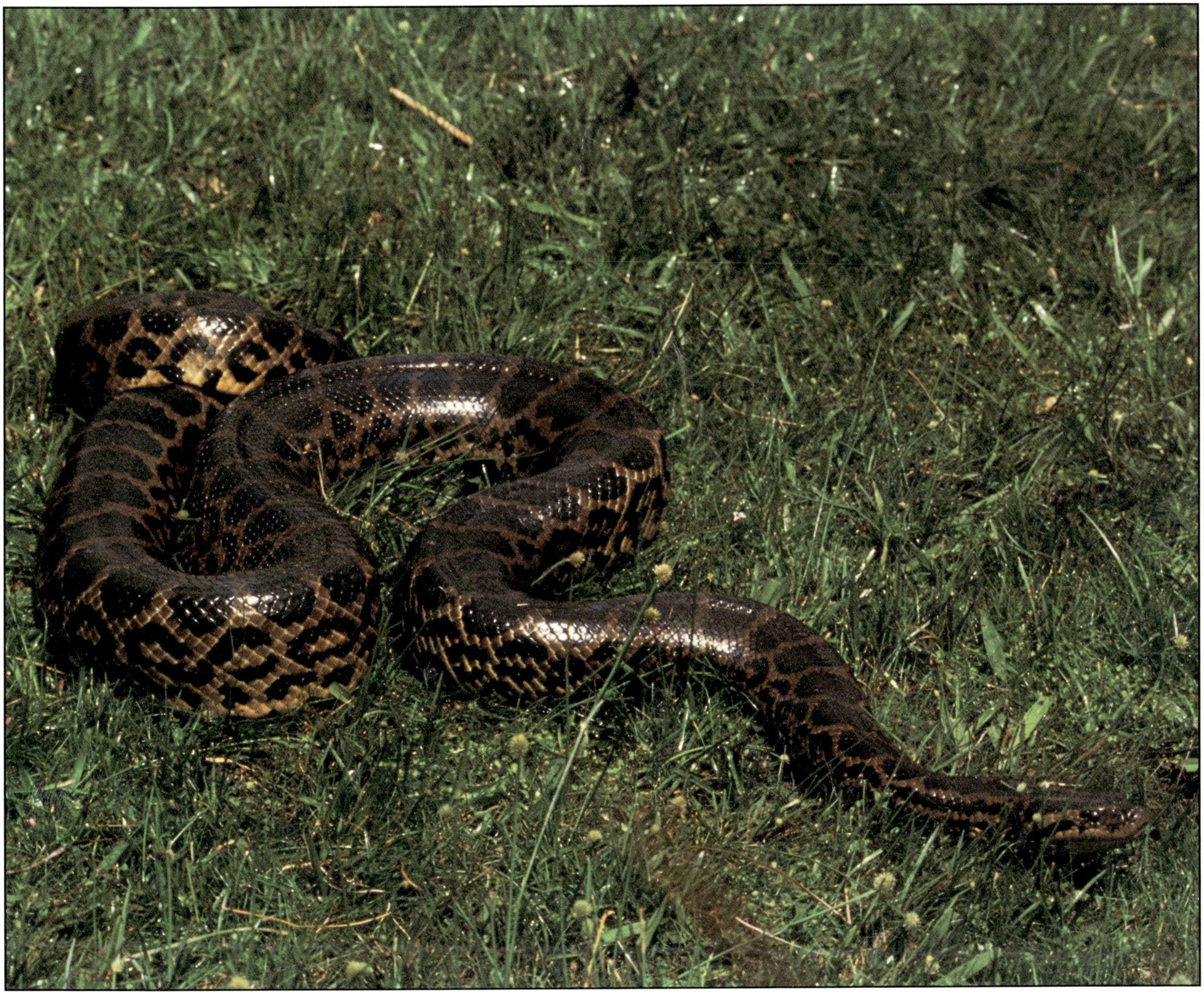

GARTER SNAKES

Garter snakes live all over North America. You can find them in the woods, in your yard, or in your garden. They are also called *ribbon snakes* because they have long stripes that run from head to tail. Garter snakes can grow up to five feet long, but they are usually much smaller. Garter snakes are not poisonous. They eat small animals like mice, frogs, and insects. Usually they will flee if threatened, but one might bite if it feels trapped. Most snakes lay eggs, but garter snakes give birth to live young—as many as 70 baby snakes might be born at one time!

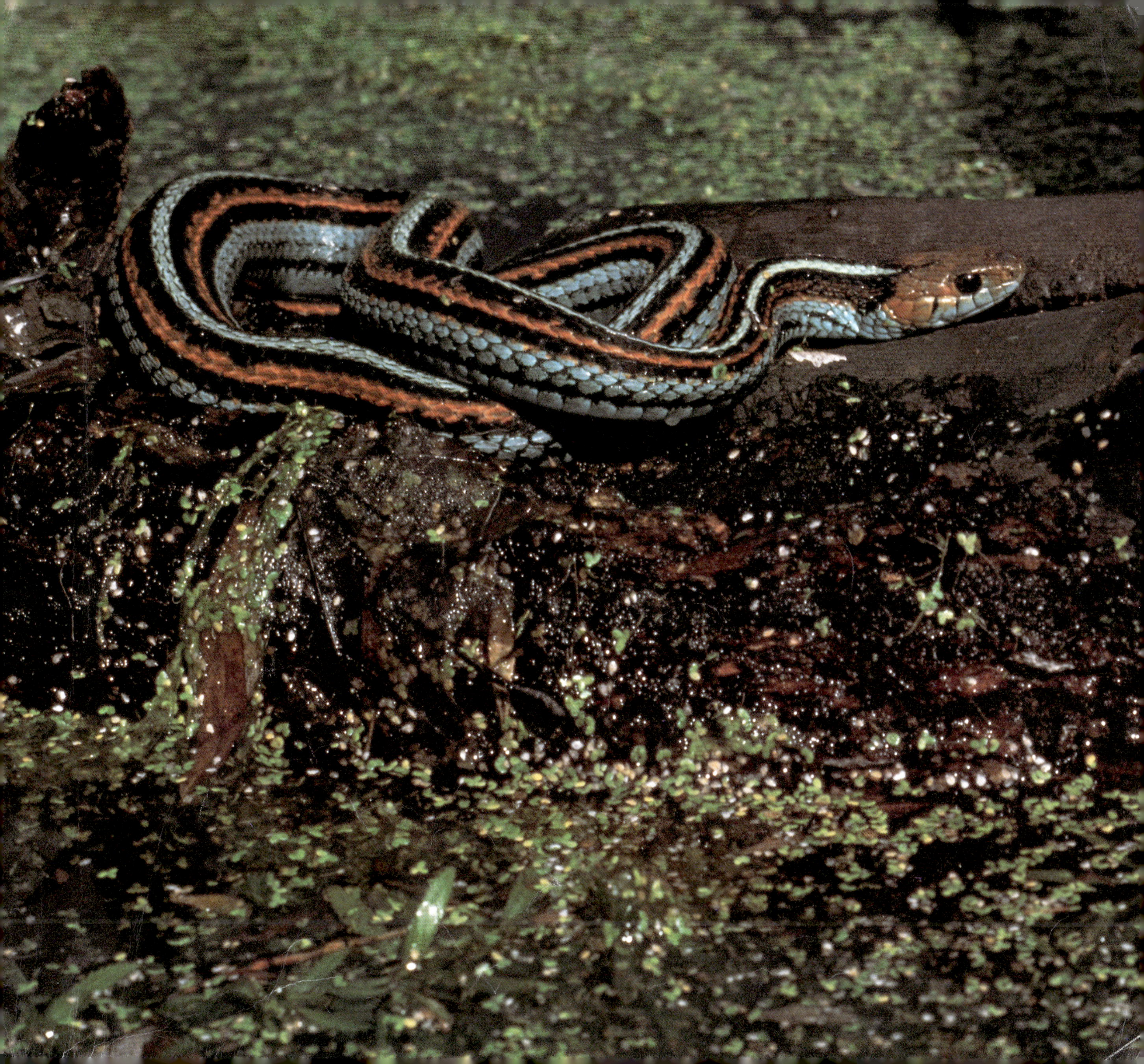

VINE SNAKES

If you saw this long, thin snake in the woods, you might easily mistake it for a vine. Vine snakes live in trees, where they are very difficult to see. They are found in parts of Arizona, Mexico, and Central America. Some vine snakes are brown, like the one in the picture, and others are green. The vine snake hunts lizards in the trees or on the ground. It is a rear-fanged snake, which means it has poison fangs at the back of its mouth. The bite of the vine snake is painful and can cause swelling and numbness, but it is not deadly to humans.

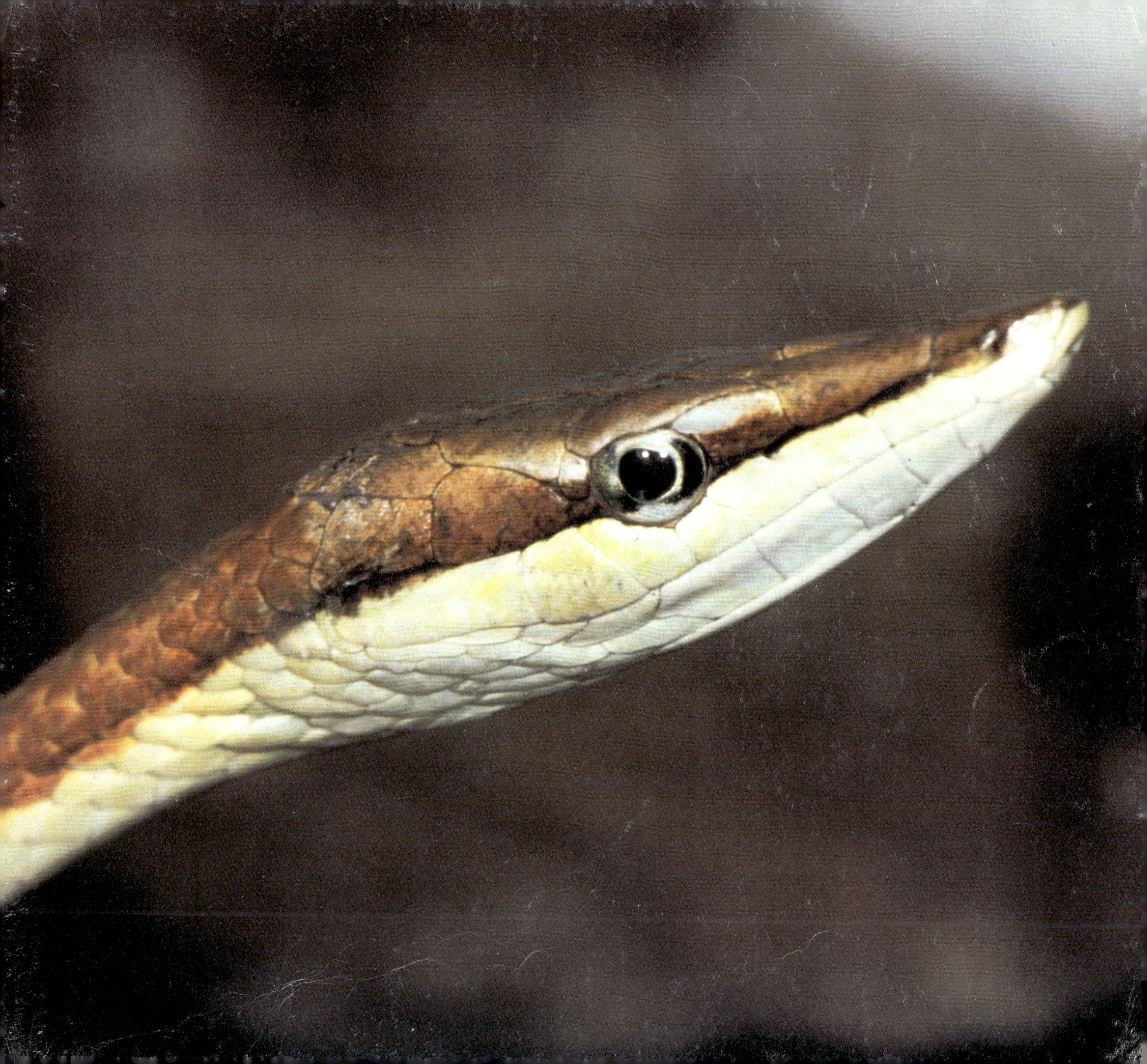

COPPERHEADS

You can recognize the copperhead by its copper-colored head and eyes. Copperheads belong to a family of poisonous snakes called *vipers*. Vipers have two large, hollow fangs at the front of their mouths. When the viper closes its mouth, the fangs fold up. When it strikes, the fangs unfold and stab deep into the snake's prey, injecting it with poison. Copperheads are one of the most common poisonous snakes in the eastern United States. They grow to about four feet long. Copperhead bites are painful but not deadly.

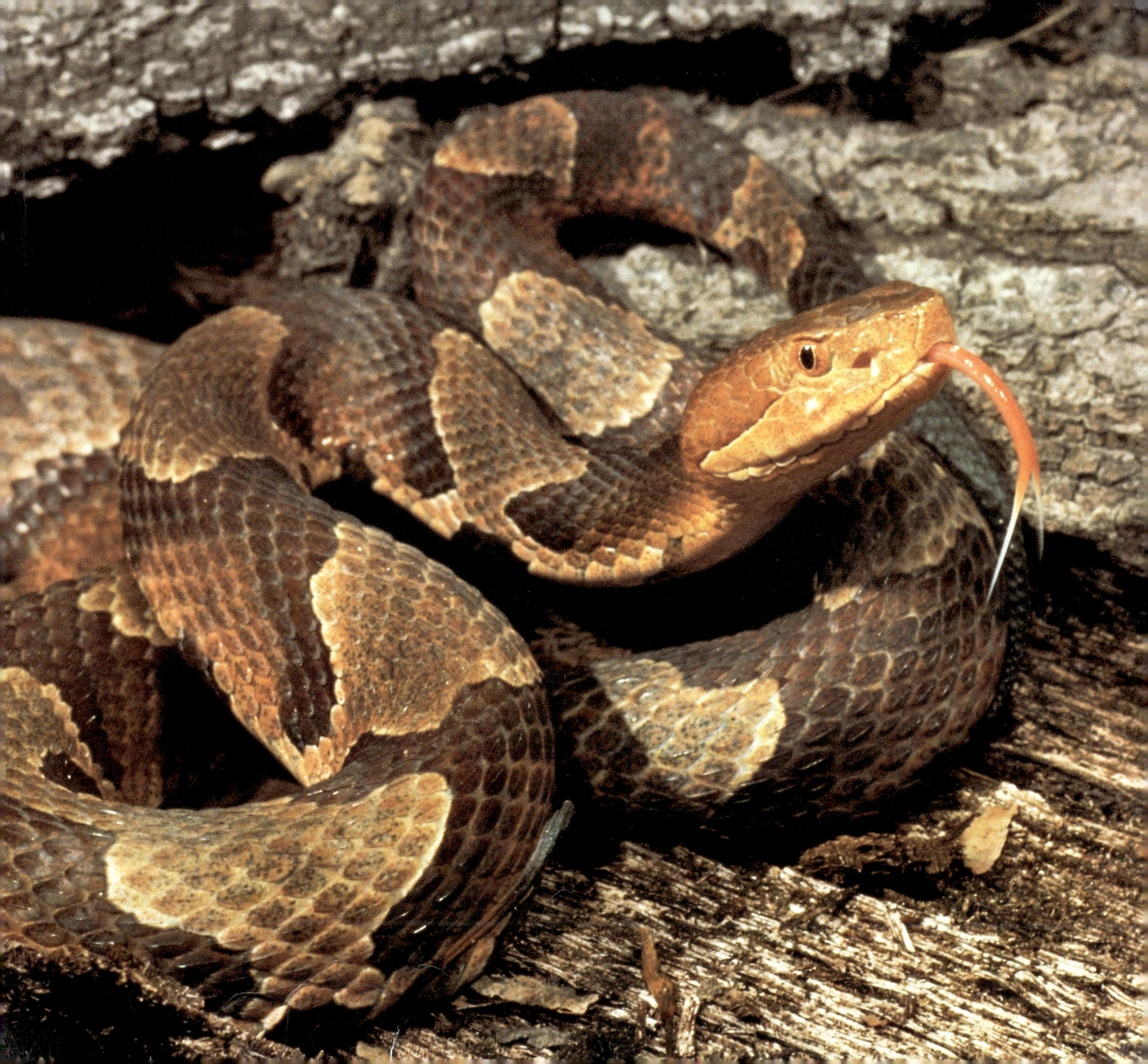

COTTONMOUTHS

Also known as *water moccasins*, these poisonous vipers are found from Florida to Texas. They look a lot like copperheads, but they are darker colored, larger, and usually live in the water. Cottonmouths eat all kinds of small animals. A young cottonmouth will sometimes wave the yellow tip of its tail to lure a frog or toad. Adult cottonmouths are aggressive and dangerous snakes. When a cottonmouth feels threatened, it will sometimes open its jaws wide, showing the cotton-colored inside of its mouth. That is how it got its name.

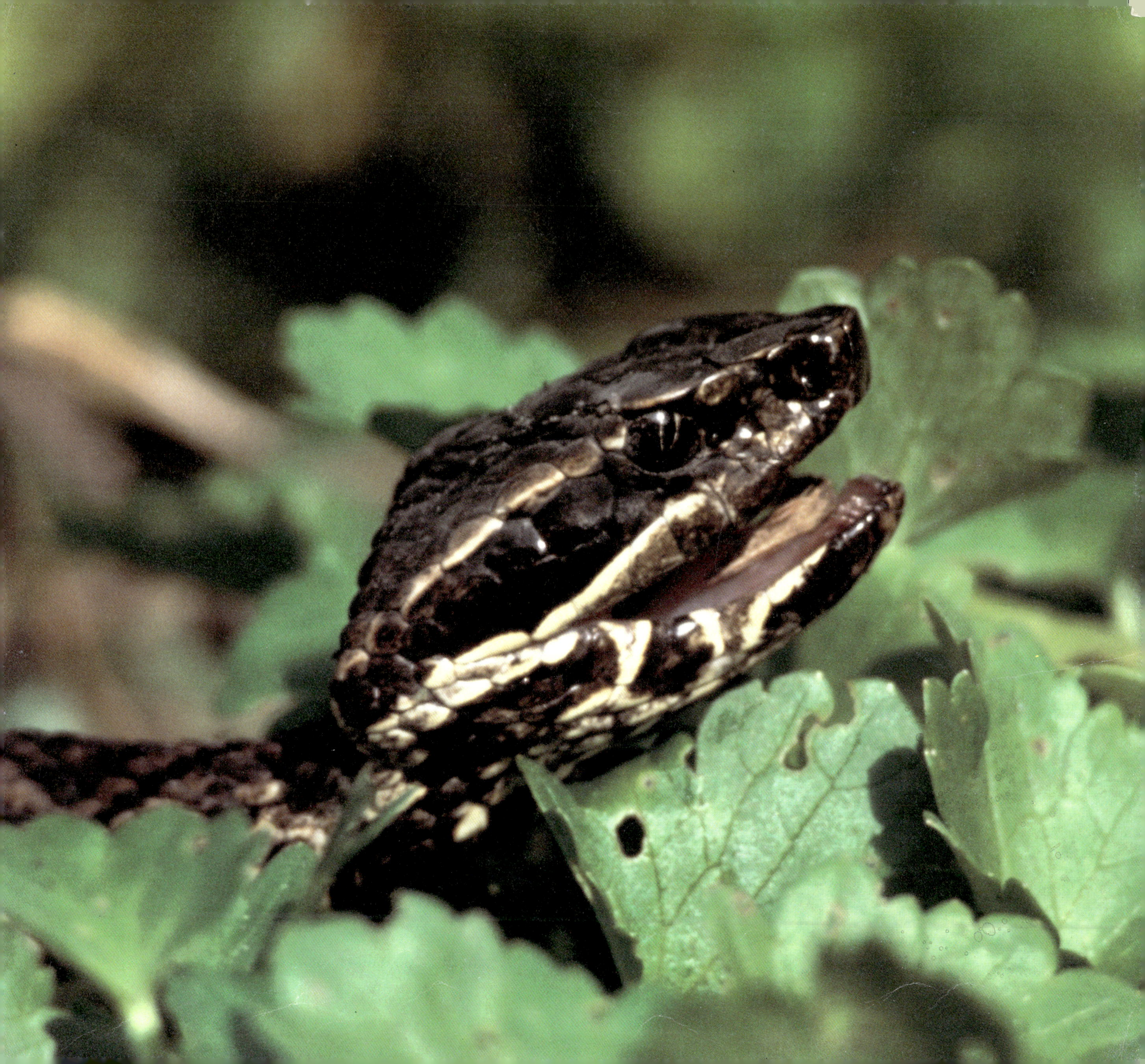

RATTLESNAKES

Rattlesnakes are another kind of viper. They are easy to recognize by the rattles at the end of their tails. The rattle is made of hollow, horny buttons. Every time the rattlesnake sheds its skin, it gets a new button. When a rattlesnake is disturbed, it coils up and shakes its tail, making a buzzing sound that means get away! The diamondback rattlesnake can grow over six feet long. It is the largest and most dangerous rattlesnake in North America. A bite from a diamondback rattlesnake can cause death if it is not quickly treated.

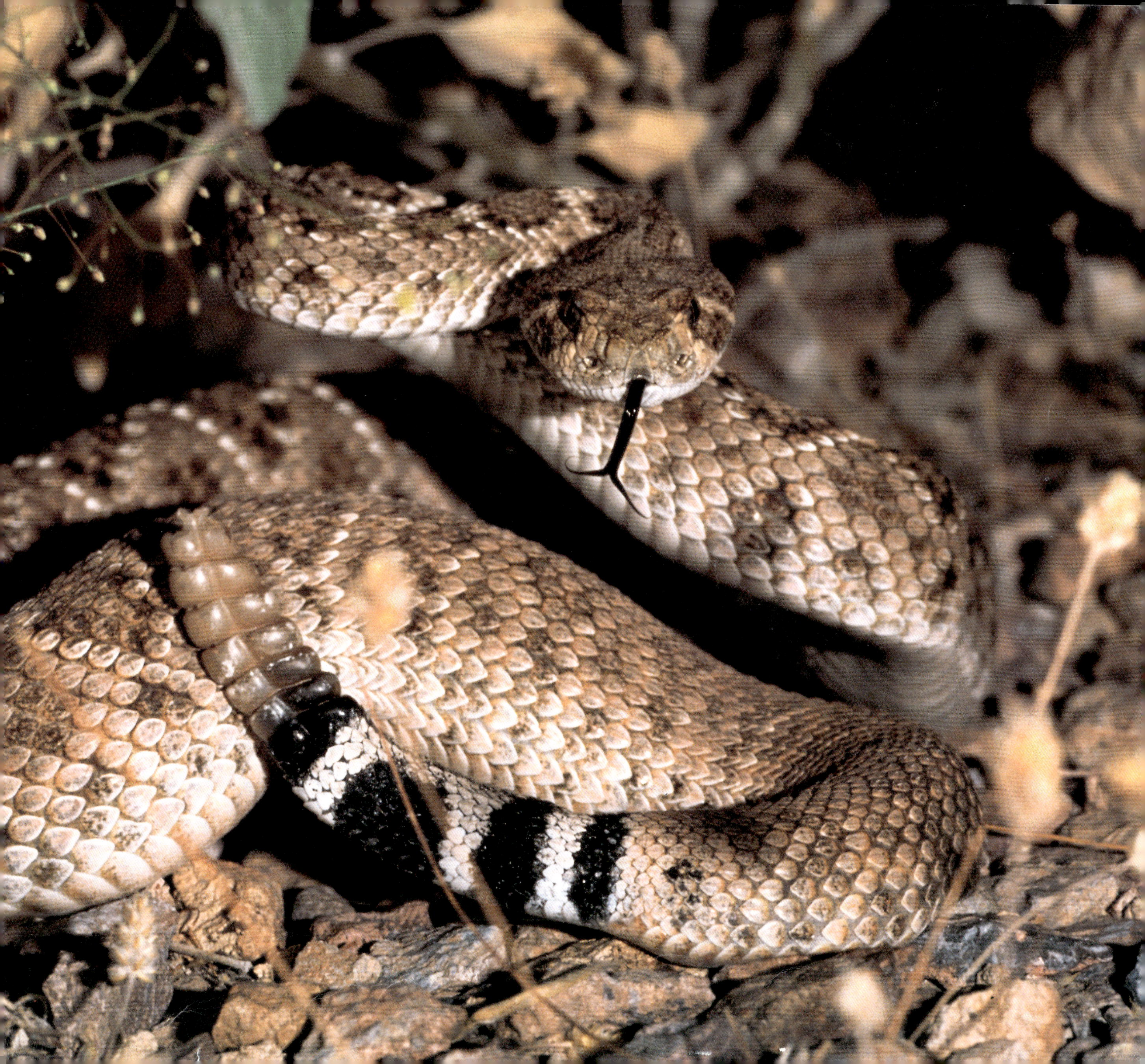

PUFF ADDERS

The puff adder lives in Africa. It is a thick-bodied, poisonous viper that grows about four feet long. Puff adders eat rats and other rodents. They strike with their fangs, then wait for the rodent to crawl away and die. After a few minutes, the puff adder follows the rodent's trail, using the tip of its tongue to test the ground. The snake uses its long fangs to pull the dead rodent into its mouth and swallow it whole. The puff adder is well camouflaged. People are sometimes bitten because they accidentally step on one. Puff adder venom is extremely poisonous.

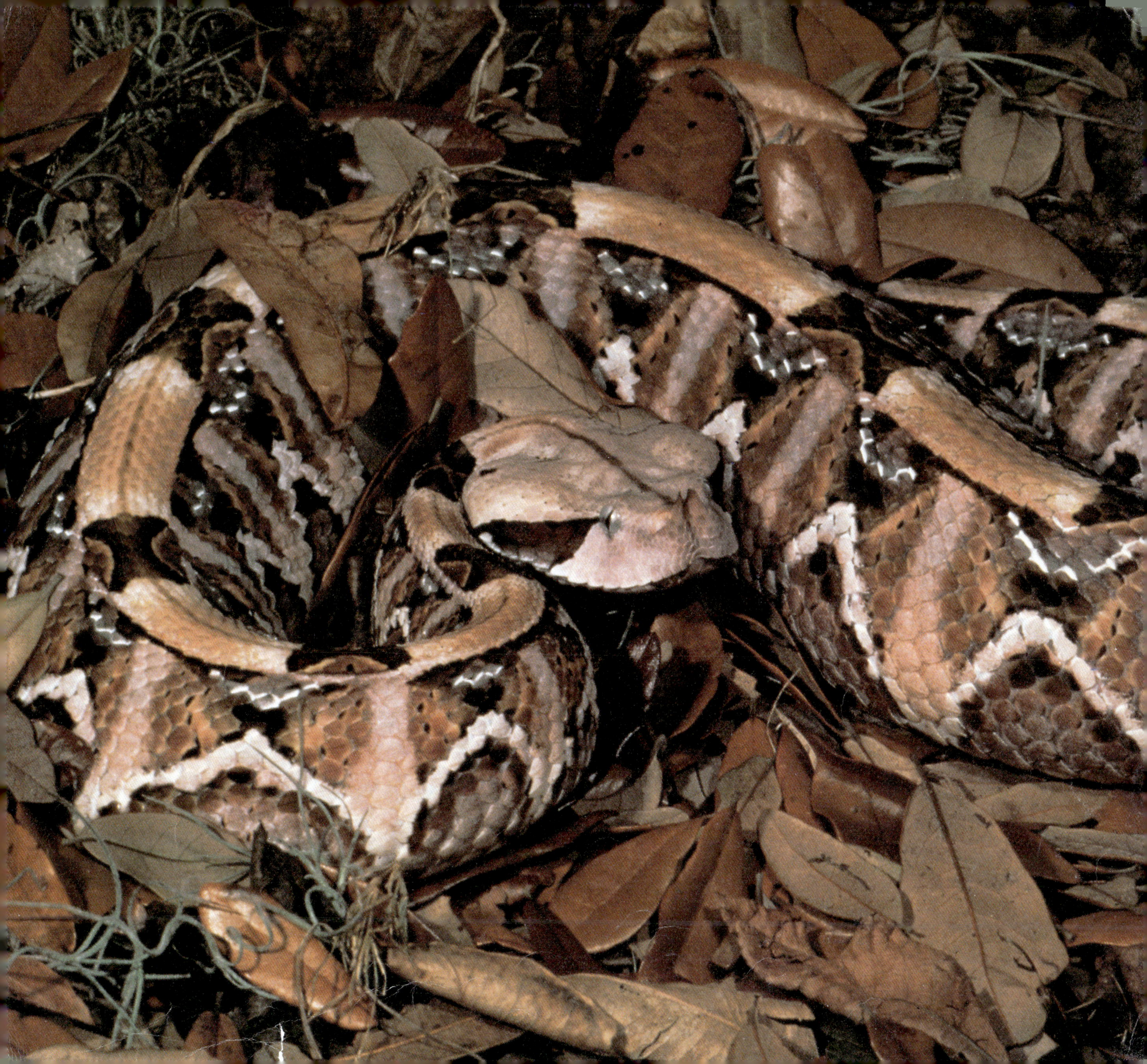

COBRAS

Cobras live in Africa, India, and Southeast Asia. They have a hood that spreads open when the snake is disturbed. The hood makes the snake look bigger than it actually is. Cobras are front-fanged snakes. They have hollow fangs like the vipers, but their fangs are much shorter and do not fold up. Cobra venom can cause death quickly. Thousands of people die every year from cobra bites. The snake in the picture is a black-necked cobra. When threatened, this African cobra can spit its venom into the eyes of an attacker.

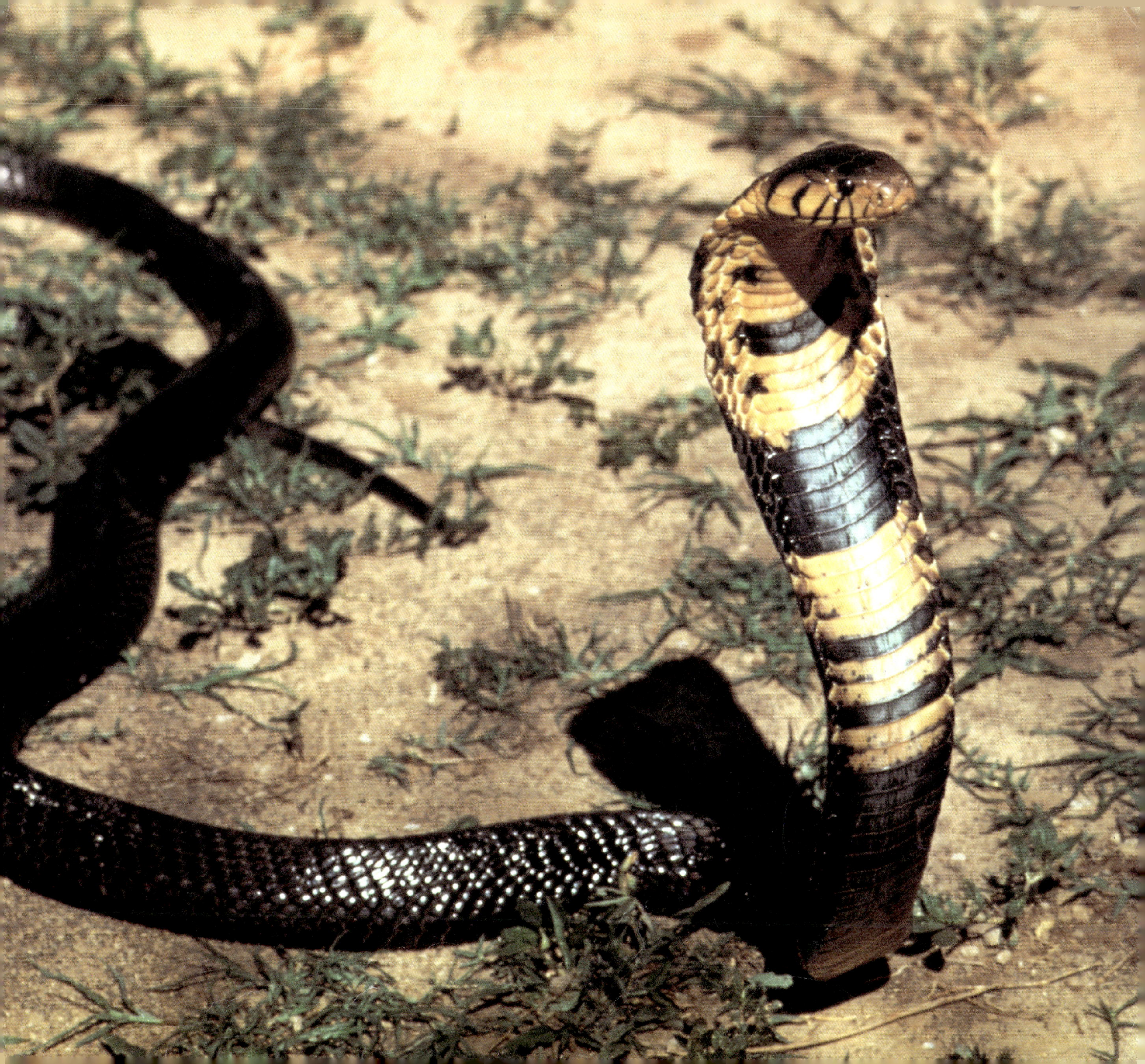

MAMBAS

Mambas are relatives of the cobras. They are front-fanged snakes that produce a very poisonous venom. The black mamba is one of the fastest, longest, and most dangerous snakes in the world. It has a long, thin body that grows up to 14 feet long. Black mambas can race across the ground at speeds of up to nine miles an hour. That's almost as fast as you can run! Black mambas live in trees and on the ground. They are aggressive snakes, and have been known to attack people. A related snake, the green mamba, is smaller and less dangerous.

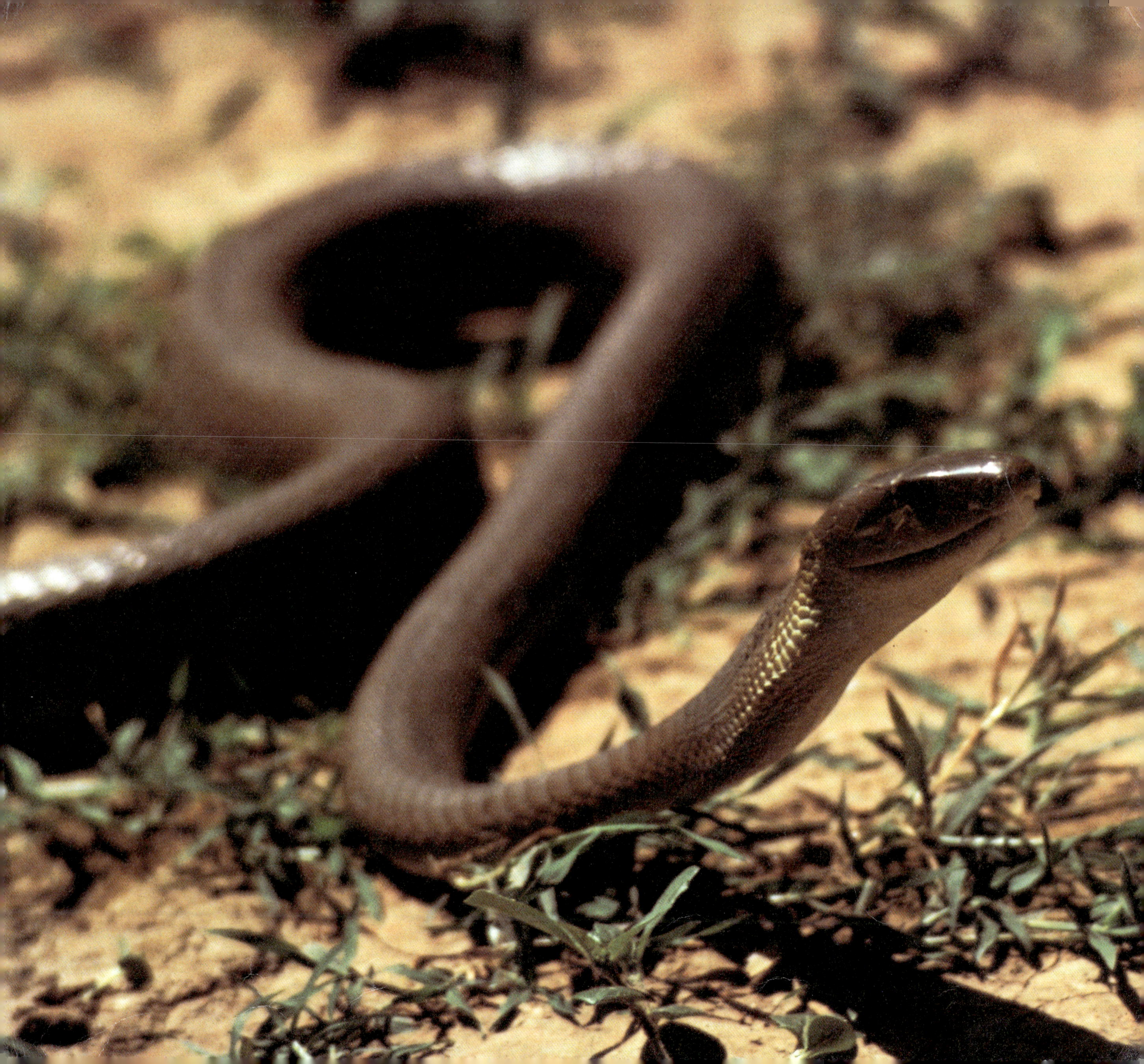

CORAL SNAKES

Coral snakes are also relatives of the cobras. They are the only front-fanged snakes found in the United States. Coral snakes are small, but their venom is very poisonous, so their bite can be dangerous. The Arizona coral snake shown in the picture spends most of its time underground. It grows to about 20 inches long. The eastern coral snake has the same red, yellow, and black markings, but it is a few inches longer. Coral snakes feed mostly on small lizards. They are shy snakes, and are rarely seen during the day.

THE CHILD'S WORLD
NATUREBOOKS

Wildlife Library

Alligators *Musk-oxen*
Arctic Foxes *Octopuses*
Bald Eagles *Owls*
Beavers *Penguins*
Birds *Polar Bears*
Black Widows *Primates*
Camels *Rattlesnakes*
Cheetahs *Reptiles*
Coyotes *Rhinoceroses*
Dogs *Seals and Sea Lions*
Dolphins *Sharks*
Elephants *Snakes*
Fish *Spiders*
Giraffes *Tigers*
Insects *Walruses*
Kangaroos *Whales*
Lions *Wildcats*
Mammals *Wolves*
Monarchs *Zebras*

Space Library

Earth *The Moon*
Mars *The Sun*

Adventure Library

Glacier National Park *Yosemite*
The Grand Canyon *Yellowstone National Park*